NOT! THE 1984 OLYMPICS

~an incomplete guide.

by TOM HEPBURN illustrations ROD PROUD

Willow Books

William Collins Sons & Co Ltd

LONDON – GLASGOW – SYDNEY – AUCKLAND – TORONTO – JOHANNESBURG

Acknowledgements
Concept and Text: Tom Hepburn
Illustrations: Rod Proud
From a bucolic thought by Paul Bradwell
Typography and Production: Selwyn Jacobson
Typeset in Cairo by
Jacobsons Graphic Communications Group
Printed by Colorcraft Ltd Hong Kong

First published in Great Britain in 1984 by
Willow Books Ltd
William Collins Sons and Co. Ltd
London — Glasgow — Sydney — Auckland
Toronto — Johannesburg

©Text: Tom Hepburn 1984
©Illustrations: Rod Proud 1984
ISBN 0 00 218139-8

Contents

WE HAVE A PROBLEM!

A Brief History — Ancient & Modern

The first Olympic Games were held, tradition has it, some 2760 years ago in the balmy climes of Ancient Greece.

Since then a few subtle changes have taken place.

A few more sports have crept into the official list, a few more countries have demanded participation, a few more rules regulate the contestants.

But certain basics remain, as this brief revue of things Olympic shows. Designed with equal disdain for the athlete, the official and the armchair critic, this book is guaranteed to teach you almost nothing about anything. You can rest assured, though, if it doesn't help you raise a barbell, it'll surely make you raise a smile!

Finally, a word on accuracy, whatever that is.

Statistics, that insidious raison d'être of sport, are virtually absent here.

Rather we concentrate on that primal motivating force of healthy competition, exemplified in the singular attribute common to all competitors — <u>the love of gold!</u>

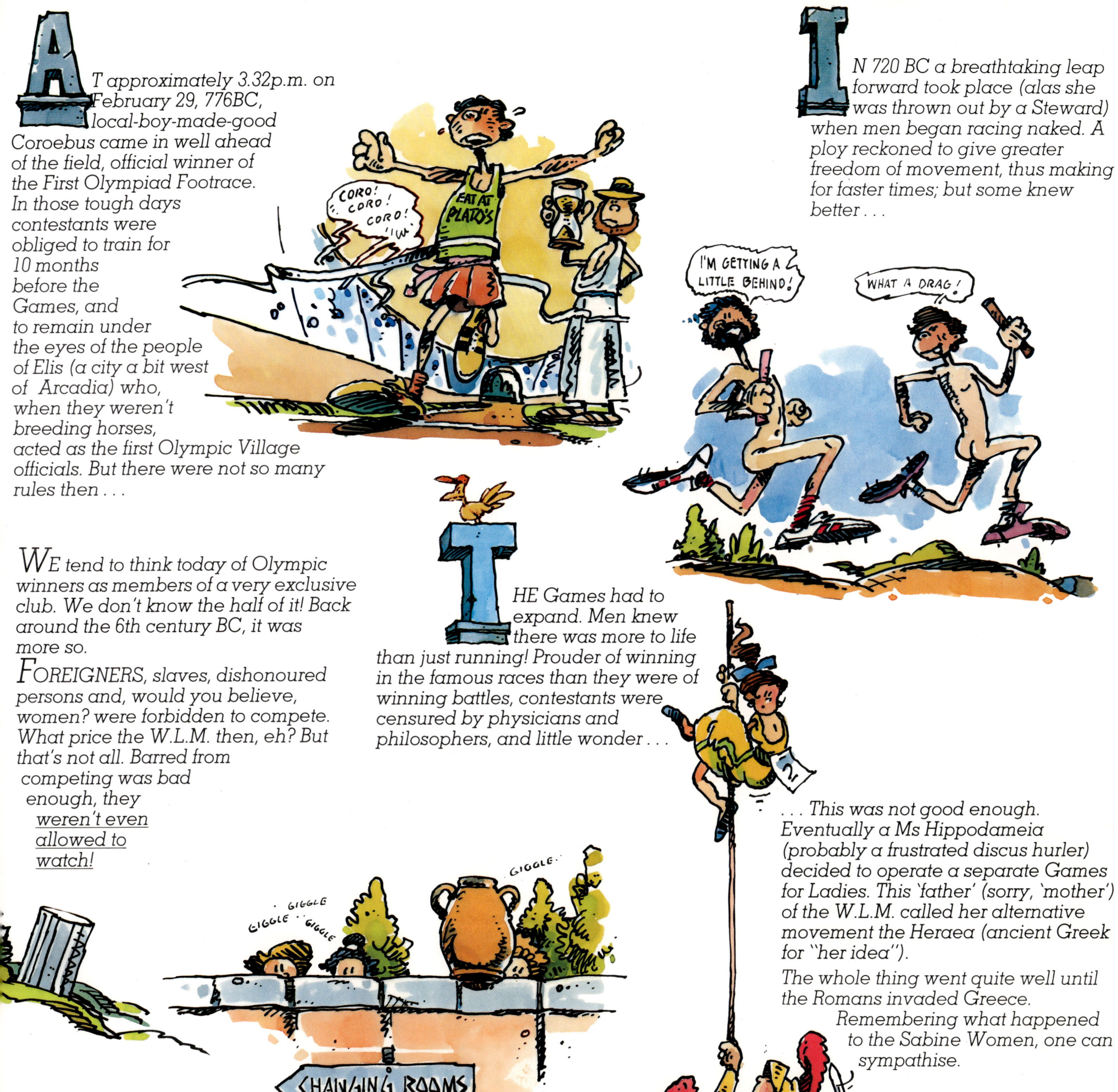

AT approximately 3.32p.m. on February 29, 776BC, local-boy-made-good Coroebus came in well ahead of the field, official winner of the First Olympiad Footrace. In those tough days contestants were obliged to train for 10 months before the Games, and to remain under the eyes of the people of Elis (a city a bit west of Arcadia) who, when they weren't breeding horses, acted as the first Olympic Village officials. But there were not so many rules then . . .

CORO! CORO! CORO!

EAT AT PLATO'S

WE tend to think today of Olympic winners as members of a very exclusive club. We don't know the half of it! Back around the 6th century BC, it was more so.

FOREIGNERS, slaves, dishonoured persons and, would you believe, women? were forbidden to compete. What price the W.L.M. then, eh? But that's not all. Barred from competing was bad enough, they <u>weren't even allowed to watch!</u>

GIGGLE GIGGLE GIGGLE GIGGLE GIGGLE

CHANGING ROOMS

IN 720 BC a breathtaking leap forward took place (alas she was thrown out by a Steward) when men began racing naked. A ploy reckoned to give greater freedom of movement, thus making for faster times; but some knew better . . .

I'M GETTING A LITTLE BEHIND!

WHAT A DRAG!

THE Games had to expand. Men knew there was more to life than just running! Prouder of winning in the famous races than they were of winning battles, contestants were censured by physicians and philosophers, and little wonder . . .

. . . This was not good enough. Eventually a Ms Hippodameia (probably a frustrated discus hurler) decided to operate a separate Games for Ladies. This 'father' (sorry, 'mother') of the W.L.M. called her alternative movement the Heraea (ancient Greek for "her idea").

The whole thing went quite well until the Romans invaded Greece.
Remembering what happened to the Sabine Women, one can sympathise.

PLACEGETTERS in the Olympics — and indeed the Heraea — were suitably rewarded. With chaplets of wild olive, no less. But back home in Sponsors-Ville, gifts and privileges were lavished upon the successful few.
As mentioned earlier, certain things are basic, and don't change too much!

LET THE GAMES BEGIN!

BARON C.

TAKE A WRONG TURN AT THE PARTHENON AND THERE'S A FEW DRACHMAS IN IT FOR YOU!

FROM the Emperor Theodosius, late of the 4th cent. A.D. to Pierre, baron de Coubertin, later still of the 19th is but a step, or rather a hop, step and jump, of 1400 odd years. The modern revival of the Games is as much due to 'Stony' Coubertin (as his friends liked to call him) as the demise of the old Games was due to Theo 1st, who had done quite well against the Visigoths but let it go to his head.

THE GAMES ARE AT AN END!

THEO

TELL THAT TO THE LION!

SINCE the first foot race back in 776 BC, the Olympic Games have witnessed many changes. Over 20 sports, and more being added every year. More money spent on a single Games than the G.N.P. of Ancient Greece for any three centuries B.C., I wouldn't be surprised. But before we speculate on where it will all end (if indeed it ever does), let us have one quick glimpse into the future, then it's on to Los Angeles 1984, and all you need to know about the Games.

Choosing a Sport

There are about 25 sports to choose from at Los Angeles this year, depending on how many you attribute to Athletics.

Study your body carefully (see below) and decide in which direction your physical prowess extends most naturally. Hold your trousers firmly. Take a deep breath. Good luck!

Who Can Play?

Any man or woman is eligible to compete in the 1984 Olympics, providing a few simple rules are observed. Like coming from a country that's been invited, being in superb physical shape, having innate talent of some kind, specialising in one of the acceptable sports for many years, finding a great coach, bettering standard entry times and having a private income large enough so's you don't have to worry about losing your job. (In some countries, we won't mention which, this last isn't really a problem!)

New Event!

We are proud to present in this volume the first announcement of a <u>New Event</u> on the 1984 Olympic calendar.

In order to trim costs and get the Games moving along at a suitable speed to justify increased charges for TV coverage, the organisers have decided to amalgamate two previously rather boring events.

<u>Not</u> a new event!

A typical Pentadecathlete

Thus the Pentathlon and the Decathlon now become the PENTADECATHLON. And what's more all 15 sports will be run simultaneously.

You can rely on something new at Los Angeles!

Archery

Who was the First Archer?
Undoubtedly a hunter, using a supple stick and perhaps animal gut or strong reed, with a burnt wood arrow head.

Then came the military: Henry V may well have ended the days of True Chivalry when his Longbowmen routed a strong French army at Agincourt in 1415. Though the French may have been partly responsible . . .

And finally, sport. From Robin Hood to Mrs M.C. Howell the bow and arrow have provided many prizes. One thing is sure, though; today's sophisticated weapon would be strange indeed to our paleolithic inventor.

Athletics

Athletics, or Track and Field, involves running, leaping and throwing things and is succinctly summarised on our cover.

The "professional foul"...

I KNOW WE SAID GIVE THEM THE BELL! BUT...

On these two pages we illustrate the highest competitor and the lowest intellect, demonstrating the hidden dangers which lurk in wait for every athlete, no matter what the sport.

Sometimes officialdom in an excess of zeal can confound the fittest of competitors; sometimes athletes themselves can be guilty of the 'professional foul' — just enough to give an edge during a closely run race.

Even that most beloved of accessories, the lucky charm (without which a competitor can feel quite naked) can offer problems. At least, a rabbit's foot can be secretly stroked and left in the locker. But lucky shorts???

Basketball

An official Olympic sport since 1936, Basketball was originated in 1891 by 'Big Jim' Naismith not a million miles from the Springfield (Mass.) YMCA.

It is a surprising fact that it took until 1951 before investigations (and convictions) were instigated for 'fixing'.

In this game exceptionally tall men throw a ball through a metal hoop for exceptionally large sums of money. There have been many great Basketball players, very few of them South Korean. The Chamberlain brothers, Neville and Wilt, spring to mind.

Taking advantage of the count

Boxing

Mentioned by Homer and included in the original Olympic Games, boxing is one of the oldest forms of competition known to man.

The major difference between professional (up to $100 million a fight for the winner these days) and amateur (Olympic!?) is that in the Olympics the fighters actually try to hit each other.

Oscar Wilde's friend Alfred's father, who had rather a thing about big strong men making each other bleed, came up with a few rules, including the still popular mandatory count of 10 seconds after a knockdown. Many boxers find this gives them time to reassess their situation.

Despite appearances to the contrary, many fighters are good friends outside the ring!

WELL, I NEVER...

GOOD LORD, KENNY ISN'T IT?...

IT'S BEEN YEARS...

AND THE REST...

HOW'S YOUR MUM?...

FINE, THANKS...YOURS?

OH, NOT SO BAD.. LEG PLAYS HER UP IN WINTER, BUT.....

SIGH?

Canoeing

Again, a fine example of necessity turned into sporting fun. From the hollowed log which allowed North American Indians to use their river systems as virtual motorways, today's craft are often aluminium or even non-sinkable rubber compounds. But even a non-sinkable canoe faces the odd problem . . .

Arnold was one who favoured the safer third wheel!

Cycling

For some reason, a sport neglected by the Ancient Greeks, doubtless because of the hazards of riding naked. But any sport where man can exceed 200kph under his own leg power (Jose Meiffret, 1962) must have its attractions. Seven champions are crowned each Games, yet strangely the safer tricycle, popular with women and shorter men, has not featured in many finals.

Diving

The art of descending without pain into water — or if you're in the Fight game (see under Boxing) — onto canvas.

One of the most graceful sports, the exquisitely tuned human form floats, twists and turns like a swallow . . .

It is not necessary to be able to swim to dive well, but competitors should endeavour to enter the water head first to gain maximum points.

MAXIMUM POINTS

MAXIMUM PAIN.

MAY I SUGGEST THAT THIS WASN'T QUITE WHAT THEY HAD IN MIND WHEN THEY WANTED YOU TO TAKE A DIVE!

SEND HIM BACK TO HIS OWN PAGE!

Equestrian

The hyracotherium (horse to you) started off about 45-50 million years ago, yet it wasn't until quite recently (the Bronze Age) that anyone thought to get up and ride on the beasts. And it wasn't until the (yes, them again) Ancient Greeks ran them in competition and the Romans raced them in teams pulling chariots (ah the thrills and spills of the Circus) that anyone even made a buck out of them! Imagine. Fifty million years and not a bet placed!

— ABOUT THIS NEW FELLA ON OUR TEAM RODNEY?

HONEST CAS

NEROS NAG 7.

PHAR LAPUS 2-1

RED RUMUS 3

And how have things developed since that dim and distant Eocene dawn? Today they run round in tight little fenced-in circles, and some people _do_ make a dollar (though not many). And in the Olympic Games they run round in even tighter little circles and jump over things.

Progress? Ask yourself. Fifty million years, and they're _still_ running around in circles?

Fencing

Often confused with Beekeeping, and equally deadly if you forget your mask, this is the only Olympic sport (introduction 1896) in which competitors have to be plugged into a power socket. This allows judges to note how many ohm runs they make.

D'Artagnan and his fellow Musketeers <u>might</u> have made gold medal standard — but one wonders how the area limits — 40' length by 6' width — would have curtailed their natural style?

Football

One of the most ancient of games, and part of the Olympic lineup since 1900, Soccer (from the Gaelic Sŏc-Hùrî, the traditional response to a nagging wife) used to be played between 22 players and one ball. Today this old fashioned form is fast disappearing, replaced with up to 100,000 screaming hooligans who divide into two factions, travel to a distant arena and for 90 minutes wage verbal and physical war on each other, officials, any footballers silly enough to venture onto the pitch, and as many railway trains and European cafes as they can find.

A typical British (?) football fan will gladly travel the world in support of his team. Including when, as here, they're not even playing!

But who cares who wins when there's a terrace to do battle on?

Kissing and cuddling and falling down for no apparent reason are encouraged, though when indulging in the last it is as well to clutch an ankle and grimace, just to add verisimilitude. Points are awarded for length of passionate embraces, time spent running behind goal posts with clenched fist raised at spectators and distance of spit aimed at the referee's back.

Recognised, doubtless because of the above characteristics, as the most popular sport in the world.

Some countries take the game more seriously than others . . .

Gymnastics

Exercises for the balanced development of the body. Not only an official sport, the Gymnasium was where the original Olympic athletes trained. Can't get closer than that to the real thing, unless you train on coke!

Gymnasties is the Science whereby nubile female children are force-fed anti-ageing drugs which turn them into even more nubile teenagers, holding them at this level so that they might corkscrew themselves into postures which command 10 out of 10 in competition.

What happens to them when they become old maids of 16 is seldom if ever made public. Do they lead normal sex lives? Can they have children? Do they ever grow up? Does anyone, watching their delightful contortions on TV, really care?

Handball

The Olympic Handball game is played with two teams of 7 on a court not unlike a football pitch. It is very fast and dominated by the Central Europeans.

Another version is the English game, played with teams of 5 (Eton and Winchester and all that).

HEY COME ON GUYS! IS THIS ALL THERE IS TO THIS GAME?...

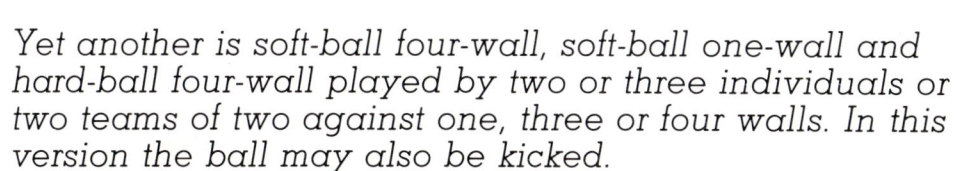

Yet another is soft-ball four-wall, soft-ball one-wall and hard-ball four-wall played by two or three individuals or two teams of two against one, three or four walls. In this version the ball may also be kicked.

This is the Irish Handball, played by them since the Middle Ages.

No, it doesn't surprise me either.

Hockey

As Marco is to Polo, so are India and Pakistan to Field Hockey. The connection between hitting a defenceless object with a stick and British Colonial Rule is clearly undeniable (viz cricket, the Black Hole of Calcutta, etc.).

Developed to its present sophisticated level largely through the influence of the St. Trinian's School of Playing Standards and the fine action paintings by English artiste David Hockey, the game we know today (an Olympic regular since 1908) bears little resemblance to the mediaeval pastime known as 'Hack-It'. Though on second thoughts . . .

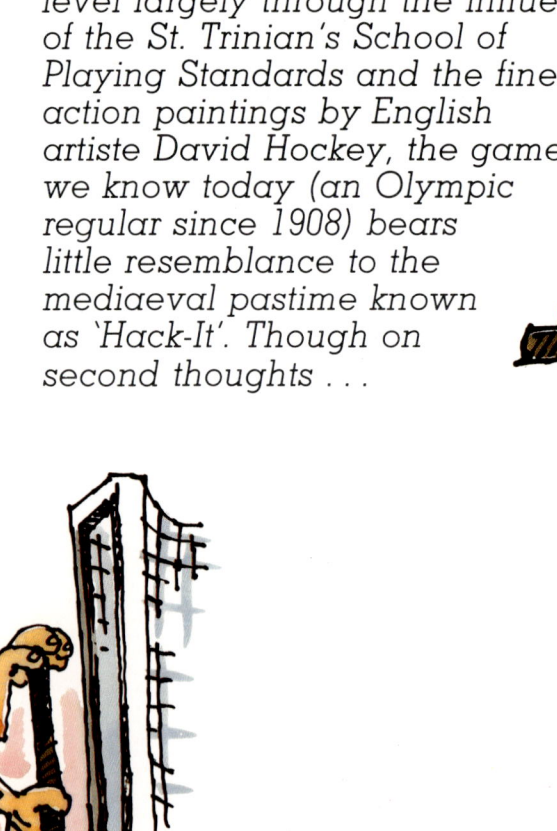

Judo

Using the weight and strength of an opponent against him is the basis of this scientific sport.

Created by Jigoro Kano in 1882 as a modified (i.e. less dangerous) version of the 2000-year-old Jiujitsu, Judo can be compared to a modern marriage.

After the initial ceremony (an exchange of vows or a formal bow) the two combatants thereupon hurl themselves upon each other and wrestle furiously until one gives in.

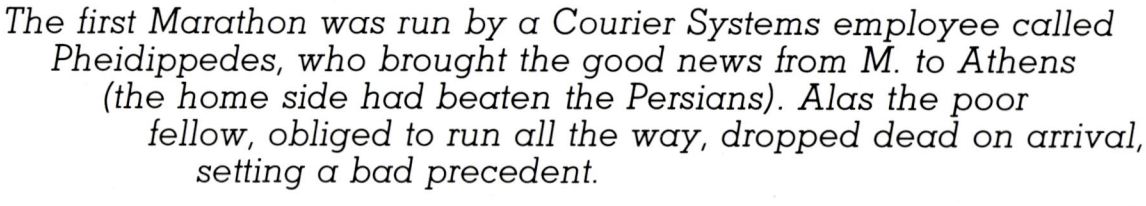

Marathon

Next to 'the magic mile', surely the most emotive event in the Olympiad! Part of the Modern Olympics since their inception in 1896 this race, symbolic of the whole Olympic concept, was not part of the Ancient Games.

The first Marathon was run by a Courier Systems employee called Pheidippedes, who brought the good news from M. to Athens (the home side had beaten the Persians). Alas the poor fellow, obliged to run all the way, dropped dead on arrival, setting a bad precedent.

Yet this untimely demise was not so surprising when one realises it was his fifth Marathon of the war — he'd been sent to Sparta four times seeking aid, a good 150km each way as the roc flies.

Rowing

The only Olympic sport (introduced at Paris in 1900) where contestants race backwards — a hangover from the sport's origins when gigantic war galleys were propelled by up to 40 banks of slaves (later convicts) who not only couldn't see where they were going, but weren't allowed to get off when they arrived. To relieve the tedium of long voyages, which sometimes lasted years, the crews would often race each other.

New Zealand and Australia are particularly good at this sport, doubtless because of their convict ancestry.

Today's hurling of the coxswain into the water after a win stems from the traditional human sacrifice (sensibly the smallest, weakest oarsman) offered to Neptune by a winning war galley.

Shooting

In Athens, 1896, the first Olympic shooting events were held. One wonders why this popular pastime (read *"My Favourite 100 Wars"* by Henry T. Kay, published by Shicklgruber & Johnstone) was left out of the Ancient Games?

This sport, like most English Clubs, is divided into various bores. Do not confuse Skeet, or Trap shooting with the Irish sport of Pigeon-Hurling, where one man throws a saucer-shaped clay object into the air and his opponent tries to bring it down with a live pigeon.

Swimming

In this, another founder member of the 1896 Modern Games, speed is once more of the essence.

The fastest stroke is an overarm style known as the Australian Crawl. Coincidentally the slowest style is also Australian and is known as the Chappell Underarm.

Swimming should be accomplished with the minimum of splashing and the least resistance to water. To this ideal many champion swimmers shave all hair from their bodies. Just to prove how much Australians dominate this sport, the shaving technique is often referred to as the 'Gunston Effect'.

The Gunston effect

The Transylvanian Tummy Tap

The Brazilian Back-heel

The Nippon Nudge

Volleyball

One of the most recent sports to join the prestigious Olympic lineup (1964), Volleyball was originated in America by Bill Morgan in 1895.

It is a game which involves a great deal of falling down — more even than Tennis or Soccer — and the Japanese excel here above most other nations. Perhaps because of their predilection for Judo, perhaps because they are a bit closer to the ground than most people.

Volleyball is a fast and furious sport where any part of the body may be used as a 'bat' to knock the ball over the net between two teams. Some of these parts are of course more suitable than others, but an inventive player can take his opponents by surprise . . .

The Bravest Shot of All!

Water Polo

A peculiar sport, being part Soccer, Football (American and Aussie rules), Basketball and Hockey. And of course, Swimming. Since much of the game is played underwater, refereeing can be a little awkward.

As in All Black rugby, choking, butting, tackling and gouging are permitted. An Olympic sport since 1900, this game is popular with, and played very well by, the Hungarians. Perhaps because of all the practice they get lobbing bombs at Russian tanks?

Weightlifting

Why are the Russians synonymous with weightlifting? (And indeed Shotputting?).

What is that secret ingredient which makes their heavyweights heavier?

Is it that permanent yoke about their necks?

Is it all that time spent pulling tractors out of snowdrifts?

Why is it so difficult to tell the men from the women?

All these questions and many more are carefully avoided in this book.

Wrestling

One of the most primitive and universal of sports, probably popular with prehistoric man. (In the Mists of Antiquity it was often hard to tell P. Man from P. Woman, and when a bloke felt like a spot of the Pleistocene other, a good fierce wrestle often served to clarify the issue.)

The Greeks considered Wrestling second only to the Discus in the Olympiads. How sad they would be could they watch the pathetic professional histrionics called Wrestling today!

Fortunately Amateur Wrestling maintains a high standard and is an exciting part of the Modern Olympics.

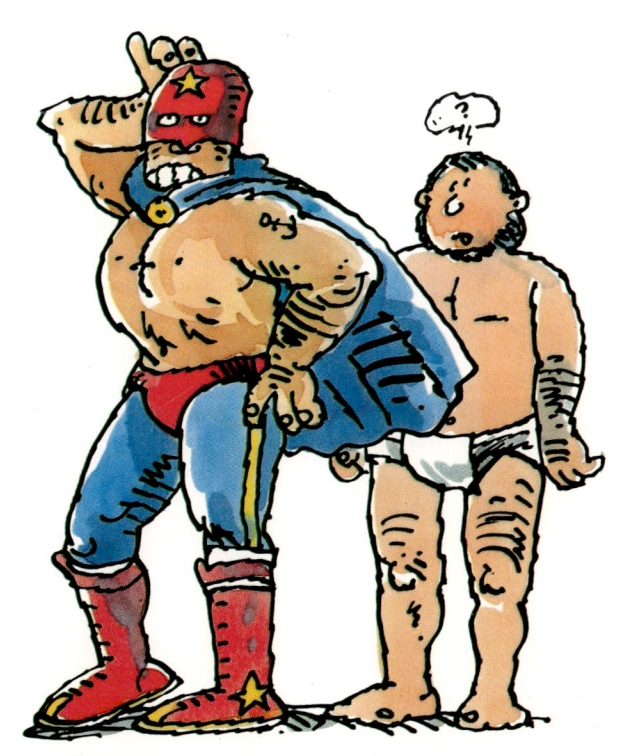

Yachting

In the humblest dinghy or the grandest cruiser, more people 'muck about in boats' than enjoy any other single sporting activity.

Be it a quiet hour's fishing or a tense international race all 'boaties' are equal . . . safe in the knowledge that power gives way to sail, large gives way to small . . .

NOT ONLY IS THIS A GREAT LITTLE FISHING SPOT,—I DO BELIEVE WE'LL CATCH A GLIMPSE OF THE OLYMPIC SOLINGS WITH A LITTLE LUCK!

Special Exhibition Sports

Tennis

Once upon a time only girls and upper-class twits played tennis. (viz. "I say, anyone for . . .?)

Now it's an official 'exhibition game' at the 1984 Olympics at Los Angeles. Well, it would be, wouldn't it? Along with Baseball it's one of the very few games the Yanks can be sure of winning.

Actually, 'exhibition' is right! The first important tennis exhibition on record was on June 20, 1788, when Louis XVI wouldn't let his Third Estate Deputies into their meeting rooms, so they gathered on his indoor tennis court instead and declared themselves the National Assembly.

This was known as 'The Oath of The Tennis Court'. These days this kind of thing is left to John McEnroe, whose oaths are second to none and can assure the USA of a gold medal whenever Tennis becomes an official part of the Olympic programme.

Baseball

This, the national game of the United States, is according to one authority derived from 'one old cat!' The 18th century children's game of the same name, mixed up a bit with a dash of English Cricket, has resulted in a cultural fixation which is to Americans as Rugby is to New Zealanders, Soccer is to hooligans and Seppuku is to embarrassed Japanese. In other words, a sport to be taken seriously; not to be trifled with; something to succeed at no matter what the cost! Sounds like fun, eh?

Perhaps this is why Baseball has been adopted as an official exhibition sport for the L.A. Olympics. Something for the locals to excel at, to show old Ivan that the only Red Sox worth wearing come from Boston, not Belorussia.

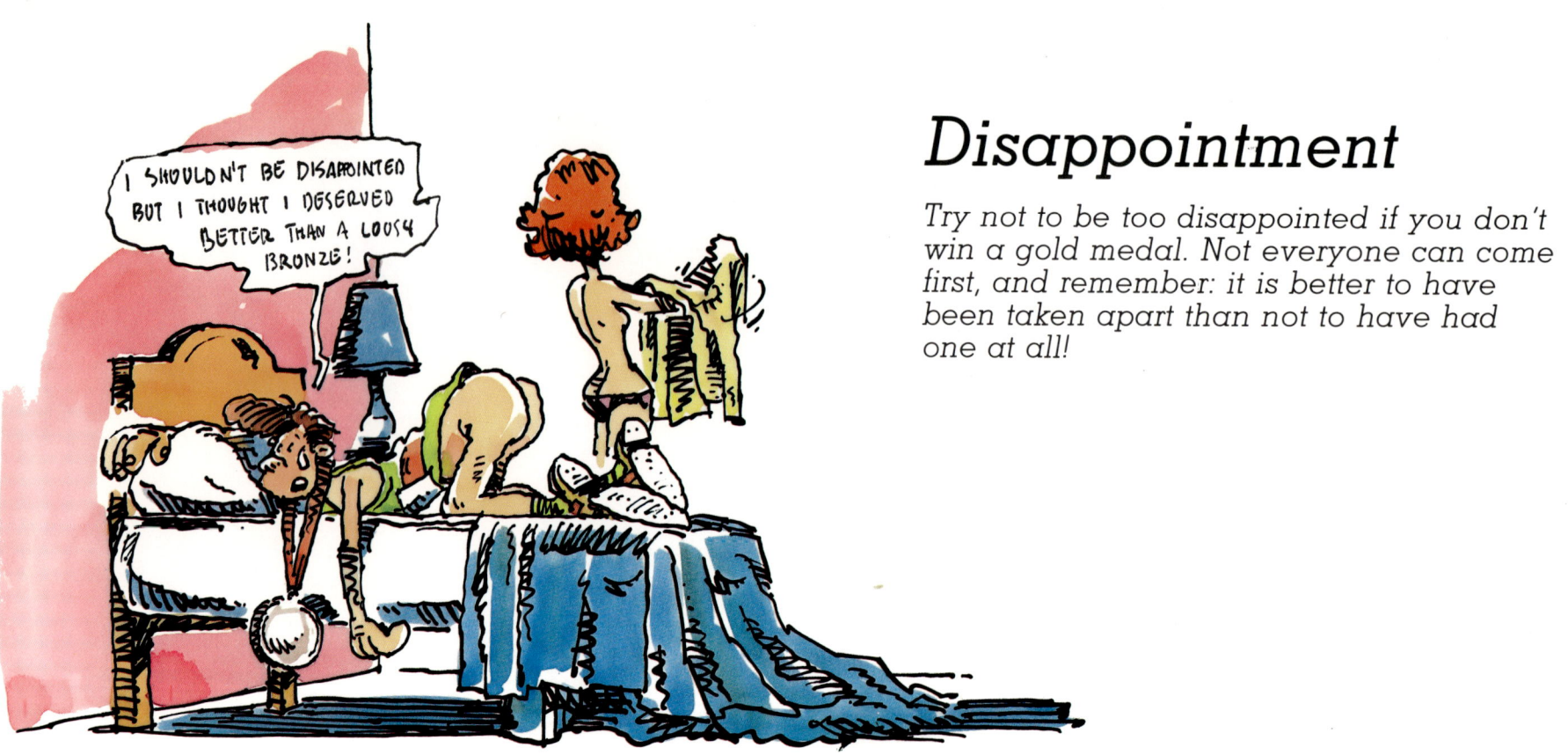

Disappointment

Try not to be too disappointed if you don't win a gold medal. Not everyone can come first, and remember: it is better to have been taken apart than not to have had one at all!

Romance

Despite the official segregation, it is often possible to make friends. Sharing a sport is a great start, you have an immediate sympathy, a mental rapport whatever the language problems, something you can truly share. Remember, in the Olympics even a Bantamweight can love above him!

Drug Abuse

With modern drugs so efficient at enhancing this or that attribute, great care is taken by the Games authorities to ensure no one competitor has an unfair advantage.

However, some stimulants are not forbidden . . .

Homecoming

Few can resist the temptation of duty free goodies, but beware the eventual cost.

What seems a great idea at the time can often mean there's more to pay than originally thought.

We all know that it's the taking part that counts, not the winning ... well, most of us know. But it isn't always easy to explain to the folks back home that you really did do your best ...

The subtle effects of a prolonged period in another country, different values, new styles, can cause the odd raised eyebrow back home.

In most cases these effects are temporary. And if they're not then there's a permanent cure ... known in some parts of the world as the 'Gulag Grind'.

The Armchair Critic

Of course, if you were only to train, sure you'd be just as good as that lot, we believe you. But meantime, what greater pleasure than to relax in front of the Box, a cool beer in your hand, and watch the world's finest athletes go for the gold? An exhausting thought, indeed.

Willow Books

Willow Books
William Collins Sons & Co Ltd
LONDON – GLASGOW – SYDNEY – AUCKLAND – TORONTO – JOHANNESBURG